CW00591748

Spanish

Spanish Within Everyone's Reach With Simple And
Practical Lessons

Marcus Rodriguez

© Copyright 2021 - all rights reserved.

The content contained within this book may not be reproduced, duplicated or transmitted without direct written permission from the author or the publisher.

Under no circumstances will any blame or legal responsibility be held against the publisher, or author, for any damages, reparation, or monetary loss due to the information contained within this book. Either directly or indirectly.

Legal notice:

This book is copyright protected. This book is only for personal use. You cannot amend, distribute, sell, use, quote or paraphrase any part, or the content within this book, without the consent of the author or publisher.

Disclaimer notice:

Please note the information contained within this document is for educational and entertainment purposes only. All effort has been executed to present accurate, up to date, and reliable, complete information. No warranties of any kind are declared or implied. Readers acknowledge that the author is not engaging in the rendering of legal, financial, medical or professional advice. The content within this book has been derived from various sources. Please consult a licensed

2

professional before attempting any techniques outlined in this book.by reading this document, the reader agrees that under no circumstances is the author responsible for any losses, direct or indirect, which are incurred as a result of the use of information contained within this document, including, but not limited to, errors, omissions, or inaccuracies

TABLE OF CONTENTS

INTRODUCTION

O ver the last several centuries, Spanish has been across multiple continents and forged connections between all of them. Spanish has persisted as a linguistic force since the Spanish empire began to cover the world over. The language spoken now isn't quite the same as the language spoken in the 15th century on the first voyage to the new world, but the similarities between that variety of Spanish and the modern-day variety of Spanish sets you up for libraries worth of literature from all over the world in the Spanish language.

What's more is the sheer beauty of the fact that Spanish, since it's covered the world over, has taken in a number of influences from other languages. Through its journey starting as a mere dialectical splinter of Vulgar Latin (the version of Latin spoken by the general populace of the Roman Republic and the Roman Empire), Spanish has picked up plenty of influences from all kinds of different languages and cultures, most notably from Arabic during the Arab occupation of Spain from the 700s to around the thirteenth century, but also from the Goths, the Basques, the Native Americans, and the Celts.

So, in other words, when you learn Spanish, you're setting yourself up to be involved in learning a whole wealth of cultural and historical information in what is a relatively passive manner. That sheer attachment to history is one of the most beautiful things about learning language in general.

However, there are a great number of reasons otherwise for which you might learn Spanish. The growth of the Latin American population and the dissemination of Latin American culture into the United States provide an excellent opportunity in two ways. Firstly, you will inevitably be a more attractive candidate for various careers from a perspective of qualifications. Your ability to speak Spanish will make you an asset in more ways than you can possibly fathom, and a huge number of companies will be lining up in order to get you to work with them, especially if you're specialized in another manner too.

Secondly, you'll have opened the door to talking to a whole new set of people. No longer will you be relegated to speaking simply to people who know and understand English; rather, you'll be able to speak to and with people from the culturally beautiful continents of South America and Central America and the wonderful Latin American people. It will also enable you to go to travel to Spain with ease and talk to numerous people who are native Spanish speakers and, more importantly, natives to the region, which will most certainly help you to understand the culture, customs, and realities of the place that you're in.

Due to many long stretches of communication with the British and as a result of normal antiquated progenitors, Spamish has offered English-speakers a genuinely simple way to bantering utilizing an alternate language. Spanish and English offer a few likenesses in sentence development. You may even understand that a great deal of Spanish and English words has comparable sounds. The restricted French sounds may in any case be natural to you in light of films and TV shows.

A portion of these one of a kind Spanish sounds incorporate the quiet "h" and the rough "r" sound; however, this doesn't totally imply that all that you watch and hear on TV is absolutely precise. In any case, having the option to receive the Spanish articulation you have procured from watching films can help you a great deal while learning the language.

Just like the English spoken in the United States, the English spoken in Australia, and the English spoken in England are vastly different, likewise is the Spanish of Spain, the Spanish of Mexico, and the Spanish of, say, Argentina. They're different in manner of accent and dialect and some basic things, such as the usage of "vosotros" in Castilian Spanish (Castellano), or the Spanish of mainland Spain, where instead "ustedes" is used in Latin American Spanish. There's also the fact that certain dialects use the pronoun vos, which is generally never used otherwise and sounds rather booky and antiquated in the same way that using the pronoun thou sound in English.

These dialects were made from the Latin language utilized by the Romans during their attacks in 1 B.C.; yet notwithstanding their normal root, the development of the Spanish language is not quite the same as the advancement of Italian and French (which despite everything share a great deal of similitudes even up to today).

This book contains demonstrated advances and methodologies on the best way to begin learning the Spanish language. I trust that through this book, you will pick up the certainty to begin learning another dialect, regardless of how old you are. Try not to stress on the off chance that you have not yet taken in any unknown dialect previously. In this book, you will locate the fundamental standards of the

9

language which can make it simpler for you to assemble expressions and sentences in French. You will learn fundamental expressions, yet additionally French letters in order, sentence development, just as articulation. There are numerous explanations behind needing to become familiar with the Spanish language rapidly. You should locate the correct inspiration and wonder why you're keen on learning Spanish. Possibly you will travel soon, or you want to serve your locale better. It may be the case that you need to upgrade your resume or, just, to extend your points of view by getting a subsequent language. Whatever your reasons, learning Spanish can be a satisfying undertaking.

Interfacing with others and our condition is the way we took in our local dialects as infants. Likewise, tuning in and associating with people around us help structure our jargon and information. The explanation that connection works when learning another dialect is that it is basic, and it's common.

There is a hypothesis in language that when learning another dialect as an intuitive procedure between a student and a local speaker, correspondence and familiarity are handily accomplished. It is on the grounds that the local speaker adjusts the language and makes it simpler for you as an apprentice to become familiar with the language. The capable speaker will utilize known jargon, talking gradually and obviously. The local speaker will modify the point, stay away from sayings, and utilize less complex linguistic structures. Thusly, the information encourages you with a superior comprehension of the Spanish language.

With more than 400 million local Spanish speakers around the world, Spanish is the official language of 21 nations and is the second most-communicated in language on the planet! Remember that you should try sincerely and focus on concentrated investigation meetings to have the option to convey in Spanish rapidly. We start by setting a practical cutoff time and making a learning plan. When you have an arrangement set up, you should begin acquainting yourself with fundamental jargon words that you can later expand upon. Next, finding an online program, guide, class, or application that will give you access to both sound and visual learning. Having a decent blend of instructional materials will assist with keeping you responsible and on target. One of the most basic parts of rapidly learning another dialect is to inundate yourself in the language as much as possible. At long last, practice increasingly visit so you can speak in light of other Spanish speakers — keeping that the objective is to comprehend the Spanish language rather than simply deciphering it.

In this book, we will concentrate on furnishing you with words written in Spanish and English. These words will be utilized in a sentence in Spanish, which we will likewise convert into English with the goal that you can investigate the setting in the two dialects. Through this, you will have the option to look at the importance of every one of the words, concentrating on only each in turn.

For example:

Hola / Hello

Hola, ¿Cómo estas? / Hello, how are you?

Here, the main word is hola, which is the word initially mentioned, while the rest of the words are what we call context. Thanks to this method, you will learn to use the main word in context and also the meaning of the secondary words.

In the following lessons, you will find words from different topics, such as verbs, adjectives, adverbs, polysemous words, home, household chores, clothes, garments, accessories, nature, animals, professions, family, relationships, numbers, and many more. Learning these words and knowing how to use them will upgrade your Spanish language to the intermediate level.

Spanish has a very different system of pronunciation to English. It's far more regular but also a fair bit more nuanced in the specific sounds. With the espoused regularity of Spanish pronunciation comes a fair amount of adjustment from our English alphabet where a given letter can stand in for any number of different sounds.

We recommend reviewing the words provided here in the book at least once every two months so that you can remember them and put them into practice in your everyday life.

There are plenty of books on this subject on the market, so thank you again for choosing this one! Every effort was made to ensure it is full of as much useful information as possible. Please enjoy!

14

15

ADVANCED WORDS AND PHRASES

Everybody knows that the most common greeting in Spanish is *"¡Hola!"*. How many times do we say "hello?" There are millions of ways to say "hi" in Spanish, too. Every one of them could be used in various situations.

Basic Greetings

You have many different greeting choices in Spanish, but you will mostly see only about eight different ones. The most common ones are:

- "¿Cómo vas?"

This is considered to be an informal way to ask a person, "How are you?"

- "¿Cómo estás?"

This is also an informal version of asking a person how they are doing or feeing. To make this a formal question, all you have to do is drop the "s" and just say: "¿Cómo está?"

- Buenas

If you are the type of person who normally says "morning" rather than "good morning," this is something you will likely say a lot.

This works much in the same way, but you can use it throughout the day, no matter if it is morning or afternoon.

18

- Buenas noches

This is considered a formal greeting that you would use when it is night. It is equivalent to "good evening" but is used when greeting someone. In order to tell somebody "good night" right before you are going to bed, you would normally say "*descansa*" meaning rest.

- Buenas tardes

If you have a meeting at two o'clock in the afternoon, you need to use this greeting. This is a formal greeting for the afternoon. How weird would it sound to greet a friend with a good afternoon?

- Buenos dias

This is a very formal and respectful way of greeting a person and is mainly used when you are greeting a person you don't know. You will use it during the morning hours.

- ¿Qué tal?

This is considered an informal greeting, and you can use it with your friends and family. It is universal for "what's up?"

Now that you know some of the most common greetings, let's look at some situations where you might use them.

1. In a Coffee Shop

Imagine walking into a café, and you see somebody you have known your entire life sitting in the corner booth, you go over and say: "*¿qué tal?*"

Why: You two are already friendly with each other, so using "*buenas*" would be too formal. You do have the option to say "hola," but this might be too boring. Good friends tend to say things like, "what's up? I haven't seen you in a long time!" So, that's why you would likely use *"¿qué tal?"* It will greatly depend on the country you are in because different countries have various words for "What's up."

2. Meeting Your Significant Other's Parents

You have been asked your significant other's parent's house for dinner for the very first time. You might be scared to death. You walk in and shake their hands, and then you would say either *"buenas noches, ¿cómo están?"* or just "buenas noches". Once the dinner is finished, you should end the evening with *"Qué tengan buena noche,"* or *"feliz noche."* If you are planning on seeing them the following day, you could also say, *"hasta mañana."*

Why: Since this is the first time you have had dinner with them, you will likely want to be respectful, so you will need to use something formal. The next time you see them, you could just use *"buenas."* If you don't have a very close relationship, don't use anything less formal than *"buenas."*

3. Texting a Person

If you are starting a conversation with someone you like or know, you could say: *"¿Qué tal?"*, *"¿Cómo estás?"* or even *"¿Cómo vas?"*

Why: These are all friendly and informal greetings. You could follow a conversation by asking something like: "How is your day going?" or *"¿Cómo va el día?"*

Basic Goodbyes

While you have many different ways to greet a person, saying goodbye is simple. *"Hasta mañana," "adiós," "chao,"* or *"hasta luego"* is all there is.

- "Nos vemos"

This is literally telling someone that "we will see each other," it is typically used when you are talking about further into the future. You would use this when you know you are going to see someone very soon.

- Chao

This word is Italian but is used as an informal goodbye. It gets used as the word "peace" in the English language. You can use it among friends.

- Adiós

This is an informal goodbye. It is normally used when making a permanent statement. When you say this, you know you won't see one another soon. This is what you would hear from a significant other when you break up.

- "Hasta pronto"

This is a semi-formal goodbye. If you know there is a chance that you are going to see them in a few days, you can use this statement; but if you aren't sure, you should use *"adiós"* or *"hasta luego."*

- "Hasta luego"

This is another formal way to say goodbye. This can be used if you are saying goodbye to somebody that you could be seeing again in a few days, but you just aren't sure when.

Here are some examples of using goodbyes:

1. Leaving Work

You have finished at work and getting ready to head home. Before you go, you want to say goodbye to your coworkers, and you will see them the next day, so you could say: "*nos vemos mañana*," or "*hasta mañana*". If it is Friday, you could say: "*nos vemos el lunes*" or "*hasta el lunes*" which means "see you Monday."

Why: These expressions are informal and formal, and that means you can use them with someone you just met: your boss or your friends.

2. At an Airport

If someone who is important to you, or you, are leaving for several months, or possibly years, this would likely be a time for you to say "*adiós.*"

Why: While you or they aren't leaving forever, it will take some time for them to come back. This is a long-term goodbye.

3. Speaking on the Telephone

While you are on the phone with a friend of yours, and you are ready to end the conversation, the most common thing to say is "*chao.*" If you are having a formal conversation, then you should use "*hasta luego.*" Why: The first option is very informal, so you should only ever use it with friends.

Spanish Slang

Let's say you are walking down the street, and you decide to walk in a bar. Inside, you see some close friends. Which of the following greetings are they are going to give you:

- "Hello, how are you?"

- "Broooo, what's up?"

When you use local slang, even the slang for "what's up," it can make a big difference.

The following are several ways to say "what's up" in 19 different countries that speak Spanish. This wasn't researched on the internet; this was done by going to countries and talking with the locals.

Colombian

- "¿Bien o qué?"

- "¿Bien o no?"

- "¿Entonces qué?"

- "¿Qué más?"

If you find yourself in Medellin, it is also said as: "*¿qué más pues?*" Those from Medellin like using "*pues,*" which means "well."

Venezuelan

- "¡Épale!, ¿qué más?"

Spanish

- "¿Qué hay?"
- "Qué tal?"

Chilean

- "Holanda"
- "Ke talka"
- "Hulax"

Argentinian

- "¿Cómo andás?"
- "¿Qué hacés boludo?"

Dominican Republican

- "¿Qué lo que?"

Costa Rican

- "Diay"
- "¿Cuál es la última?"

Mexican

- "¿Qué más?"
- "¡Quiubole!"
- "¿Qué onda?"

Cuban

- "¿Qué bola?"

Ecuadorian

- "¿Qué fue cabrón?"

Bolivian

- "¿Cómo es?"
- "¿Qué onda?"

El Salvadorian

- "¿Quionda vos?"
- "¿Quiondas macizo?"

Guatemalan

- "¿Qué onda vos?"

Honduran

- "Kiubole"
- "¿Qué pedos?"

Nicaraguan

- "¿Qué honda, chele?"

Panamanian

- "¿Qué e' lo que e'?"
- "¿Qué xopa?"

Paraguayan

- "¿Qué tal?"

Peruvian

- "¿Qué más?"
- "¡Habla!"

Uruguayan

- "¿Qué haces guacho?"
- "¿Qué haces gil, todo bien?"

FORMING SENTENCES

By now, you should have a pretty good understanding of how to form sentences of Spanish. As a reminder, it is typically okay to follow the subject-verb-object structure, but, in Spanish, it is also okay for the object pronoun to be added before your verb, or it can be added to the end of the verb if it is a command or infinitive.

Just like with English, you will place objects after the verbs. If your sentence has an indirect and direct object, you will state the direct object first:

- "Julio lee libros."

  o Libros in direct and lee is the verb

- "Margarita da comida a los pobres."

  o A los pobres is the indirect, comida is the direct, and da is the verb

There are exceptions to this rule, however. When you add in an object pronoun in place of an object, the pronoun will be placed before the verb:

- "Julio los lee."

  o Los is the direct and lee is the verb

- "Margarita se la da."

  o Da is the verb, la is the direct, and se is the indirect

Unlike with English, adjectives are normally placed after the nouns that they describe in Spanish:

- "Julio le libros Buenos"

    o Buenos is the adjective and libros is the noun

There are some adjectives that have to be placed before the noun that they are describing:

- "Julio le muchos libros."

    o Libros is the noun and muchos is the adjective

Just like in English, we have some flexibility when it comes to placing the adverbs in a sentence. Typically, you should always try to place the adverb close to the verb, but you have a few different choices:

- "Julio lee libros frecuentemente."

    o *Frecuentemente* is the adverb and *lee* is the verb

- "Julio frecuentemente lee libros."

- "Frecuentemente Julio lee libros."

Lastly, adverbs that modify adjectives should be placed in front of the adjective:

- "Julio lee libros muy buenos."

Question Formation

In Spanish, questions tend to be straightforward, and yes or no questions are the easiest to ask. Any other question you may have, you have to know the question word for it. While most questions are easy, you may have a point in your life when you have to ask or are asked a more difficult question. And nobody wanted to be having their first Spanish conversation and get asked a question that you have no clue what it means.

¿Quién?

If you are asking about a person, you will use "*quién*", but if you want to know about more than one person, you will use the plural form, "*quiénes*". If you need to convey the word "whose," you will say "*de quién*".

- "¿De quién son celulares?" – "Whose cellphones are these?"

- "¿Quiénes son?" – "Who are they?"

- "¿Quién es?" – "Who is it?"

¿Dónde?

The word "*dónde*" means where, but there are two other forms, which are based on the preposition that you use with it. "*De dónde*" means "from where" and "*a dónde*" means "to where."

- "¿De dónde eres?" – "Where are you from?"

- "¿A dónde vas?" – "To where are you going?"

- "¿Dónde vives?" – "Where do you live?"

¿Cuanta? ¿Cuanto?

These are the only question words that have a masculine, feminine, plural, and singular form. That means there are four different options when you want to ask "how much" or "how many."

- "¿Cuánto té? – "How much tea?"

- "¿Cuánta agua?" – "How much water?"

- "¿Cuántos aguacates?" – "How many avocados?"

- "¿Cuántas manzanas?" – "How many apples?"

- **I Have a Question**

There may be a time when you need to tell a person you have a question to ask. There are some ways that you can ask for permission. You can be very straightforward with *"Tengo una pregunta,"* which means "I have a question." But there are some other options.

- "¿Puedo preguntarte algo?" – "May I ask you something?"

- "Tengo una pregunta para ti." – "I have one question for you."

- "¿Puedo hacerte una pregunta?" – "Can I ask you a questions?"

- **Advanced Questions**

We all know the basic questions you can ask when meeting a person, but what if you want to ask something more than, "How are you?" Here you will find some of those more advanced questions that you can use should the need arise.

- "¿A qué te dedicas?" – "What do you do for a living?"

31

- "¿Cuáles son tus aficiones?" – "What are your habits?"

- "¿Cuál es tu película favorita?" – "What's your favorite movie?"

- "¿Hablas otros idiomas?" – "Do you speak other languages?"

- "¿Tienes hermanos?" – "Do you have any siblings?"

- "¿Tienes hijos?" – "Do you have any kids?"

- "¿Tienes alguna mascota?" – "Do you have a pet?"

- "¿Dónde creciste?" – "Where did you grow up?"

- "¿A dónde vas?" – "Where are you going?"

- "¿Estás de acuerdo?" – "Do you agree?"

- "¿Qué piensas?" – "What do you think?"

- "¿Dónde está el baño?" – "Where's the bathroom?"

Exclamation And Interrogative

The best way to share a strong opinion or feeling about something is to use expressions or words that are exclamatory. The majority of exclamatory expressions or words are similar to interrogative words.

The main difference is that, instead of asking a question, the terms will state an opinion or idea.

Here are some exclamatory examples:

- "¡Qué romántico eres!"
  - "How romantic you are!
- "¡Cuántas mentiras dice él!"
  - "He lies so much!"
- "¡Cuántas personas hay en esta centro comercial!"
  - "There are so many people at this mall!"

Using exclamatory words can take a simple sentence into a statement of pain, anger, surprise, and so on. The exclamatory word that you choose will all depend on what you want to convey and words that come after your exclamatory word. As you will notice, all exclamatory words will have a written accent, just like interrogative words.

- Qué

You will use "qué" in front of adverbs, adjectives, and nouns in order to say what or how. Here are a few exclamatory statements using "qué":

- "¡Qué rápido pasa la vida!"
  - "How quickly life passes by!"
- "¡Qué delicioso!"
  - "How delicious!"
- "¡Qué inteligentes son!"
  - "How smart they are!"
- "¡Qué mujer tan guapa!"

- o "What a beautiful woman!"
- "¡Qué casa más grande!"
  - o "What a big house!"
- "¡Qué hombre!"
  - o "What a man!"

When you place an adjective after a noun in a "qué" expression, it will generally be preceded by "*tan*" or "*más*".

- Cómo

You will always use the exclamatory *cómo* before a conjugated verb to mean how.

- "¡Cómo llueve!"
  - o "How much it is raining (or) It's raining so hard!"
- "¡Cómo celebramos durante la boda!"
  - o "How we celebrated at the wedding!"
- "¡Cómo canta esa mujer!"
  - o "How that woman sings!"
- Cuán

You should use "*cuán*" before phrases that start with an adverb or adjective, and a verb phrase always follows. It means how. It is not very common to hear *"cuán"* in regular speech and usually is only used in literary works. It is more likely that you would hear *"qué"* in everyday life.

- "¡Cuán maleducados son!"
  - "How rude they are!"
- "¡Cuán feliz me haces!"
  - "How happy you make me!"
- Cuánto

"Cuánto" should be used before verb phrases and nouns and means what, how many, how much, how, and so on. In order to modify a noun, *"cuánto"* has to match the noun that comes before number and gender. In order to modify the verb, you will always use the masculine singular.

- "¡Cuánto bailamos anoche!"
  - "We danced so much last night!"
- "¡Cuánto te quiero!"
  - "I love you so much!"
- "¡Cuántos perros!"
  - "What a lot of dogs!"
- "¡Cuántas bendiciones tenemos!"
  - "How many blessings we have!"

These are just a few ways to exclaim something in Spanish. There are several other words that you can use. Here are some exclamatory interjections that you can use.

How to express surprise

These exclamations are different ways to say things like "my god," "my goodness," or "wow."

- ¡santo cielo!
- ¡válgame dios!
- ¡ay ay ay!
- ¡madre mía!
- ¡cáspita!
- ¡pa!
- ¡córcholis!
- ¡caramba!
- ¡hala!
- ¡vaya!
- ¡híjole!
- ¡por dios!
- ¡cielo santo!
- ¡dios míos!
- ¡ah!
- ¡canastos!

- ¡cielos!
- ¡órale!
- ¡anda!
- ¡guau!

Express disappointment or anger

These exclamations are like saying "shoot" or "darn."

- ¡chale!
- ¡chinguentes!
- ¡pucha!
- ¡rayos!
- ¡caramba!
- ¡caray!
- ¡caracoles!
- ¡chuta!
- ¡mecachis!
- ¡miércoles!
- ¡maldición!
- ¡chin!

Some other exclamations

You may find that these other exclamations can come in handy.

- ¡zas! – okay or bam
- ¡como sea! – whatever
- ¡arre! – giddy up
- ¡guácala! – ew or yuck
- ¡ay! – ow, jeez, or oh dear
- ¡aguas! – look out
- ¡dale! – okay, do it, go for it
- ¡sale! – okay
- ¡obvio! – of course
- ¡pum! – bam or bang
- ¡puf! – ew or yuck
- ¡puaj! – ew or yuck
- ¡oye! – hey
- ¡cuidad! – look out
- ¡bravo! – bravo

Interrogatives

Now that you have learned how to be exclamatory, let's look at interrogatives. Interrogatives are simply questioning words, which you probably already know. Questions words are considered pronouns because they get used in place of nouns that are able to answer a question. There are 12 interrogative pronouns in Spanish, and they all have to have accent marks.

- ¿para qué? – for what purpose

- ¿por qué? – why

- ¿cuántos(as)? – how many (plural)

- ¿cuánto(a)? – how many (singular)

- ¿cuándo? – when

- ¿dónde? – where

- ¿cómo? – how

- ¿cuáles? – which one

- ¿cuál? – which or what

- ¿qué? – what

- ¿quiénes? – who (plural)

- ¿quién? – who (singular)

The majority of questions words will have exactly in English and Spanish, but there are some issues that do exist so that you use the words correctly. There are three interrogatives that mean what: *cómo, cuál,* and *qué.*

Unfortunately, you can't use them interchangeably, but some simple rules can help you to remember when you should use which.

1. Use "qué" for what when it comes directly before a noun.

"¿Qué comida comen ellos?" – "What food do they eat?"

"¿Qué libro lee usted?" – "What book do you read?"

2. "Qué" is used when it comes in front of ser when you are asking for an explanation or definition. This means when you are asking a person "What is it" or "What does it mean?"

3. "Cuál" should be used before ser when you are asking a person for a specific answer or choice. For example, look at the differences between these answers.

   a. "My address is the zip code, house number, state, city, and street name where I live."

   b. "My address is 555 Mockingbird Road, Charleston, South Carolina 11155."

The first answer would be if somebody asked for an explanation of what an address is. This would be an answer you would get for the question, "¿Qué es dirección?

The second answer is for a question like, "What is your address?" Any question that is looking to get a specific answer, just like this example question, would need the word "cuál". "¿Cuál es tu dirección?

4. *"Cómo"* is most often used in response to something when a person didn't quite understand what was said and would like it repeated. In English, if a person doesn't understand something you said, they would say "what?" In Spanish, when something like this happens, you would say *"¿Cómo?* This doesn't mean that you can use *cómo* to mean what in other situations.

It's obvious how important it is to know how to ask a person a question, but there are plenty of people who mix things up, or they just can't remember it.

Using a mnemonic device can help you to remember the proper use of a question. It helps if you can come up with your device, but here are a few that you can try out.

They are silly, and they don't give you the specific words, but they do provide your memory with a quick jolt.

"**How** did he get into a **coma**?" – Cómo is how

"**Who** dates Cindy? **Ken**." – Quién is who

"**What** do they sell at **Wal**mart?" – Qué is what

"**When** can I buy a **condo**?" – Cuándo is when

You probably already have yes or no questions down pat, and the easy question formations like, *¿Habla él filipino?"* But you can take that simple question and use interrogative pronouns to get completely different questions.

- "¿Por qué habla él filipino?" – "Why does he speak filipino?"

- ¿Cuándo habla él filipino?" – "When does he speak filipino?"

- "¿Dónde habla él filipino?" – "Where does he speak filipino?"

All you have to do is switch the subject and verb in order to get the yes or no question, and then you can add the interrogative word in front of it.

ASKING EVERYDAY QUESTIONS

Asking Questions

Here is a list of important question words. You have already learned some of them as you go along, so those should be a review. Study the pronunciations and meanings below then read some common questions you can make with them.

Qué /kay/- what

Quién /kee-in/- who

Cuándo /cwan-do/- when

Cuánto /cwan-to/- how much/how many

Cómo /co-mo/- how

Dónde /don-day/- where

Por qué /por-kay/- why

¿Qué te gusta hacer?

Me gusta mirar la televisión y andar en bicicleta.

¿Cuánto cuestan las fresas?

Las fresas cuestan diez dólares.

¿Quién es?

Es mi amiga, Sara.

¿Cómo estás?

Estoy mal.

¿Cuándo es la reunión?

La reunión es a las cuatro.

¿Dónde estás?

Estoy en el parque.

¿Por qué tienes un libro?

Porque necesito estudiar.

Because *"porque"* is both because and why, you can answer questions that use *"porque"* with *"porque."*

If you are asking a "yes" or "no" question, you just say the sentence as you would a declaration. The only thing that changes is your inflection. There is no "is" or "does" to be put at the front to make it into a question. Look at the sentence and question examples below.

Marta es mi amiga. -I am declaring that she is my friend, telling people what I already know.

¿Marta es mi amiga? -At the end of this sentence, your voice should go up slightly to indicate that it is a question.

Es mi amiga Marta. -The subject can be a bit fluid in Spanish, and this is another perfectly fine way to state the fact.

¿Es mi amiga Marta?- Because you can state the fact like this, you can also ask the question like this.

No tienes hermanos.- I am stating a fact. You don't have siblings.

¿No tienes hermanos?- Now, I am asking.

In English, we use similar inflection when asking questions, so recognizing the spoken question should not be too difficult. Recognizing a written question is also made easy by the question mark at both the beginning and the end of a question.

Activity 1. Read the following situations and write a question for each one. Suggested questions are given below. You can also write example answers.

1. You want to know if your friend has your favorite food.

2. You want to know where your dad is.

3. You want to know when your Spanish class is.

4. You want to know how much something costs.

5. You want to know who the girl is.

Answers:

1. ¿Tienes carne?

Si, tengo carne.

2. ¿Dónde está mi padre?

Tu padre está en su trabajo.

3. ¿Cuándo es mi clase de español?

Es a las tres y media.

46

4. ¿Cuánto cuestan los huevos?

Cuestan ocho córdobas.

5. ¿Quién es la niña?

La niña es mi hermana.

Activity 2. Write answers for the following questions. Suggested answers are written below.

1. ¿Quién eres?

2. ¿Qué te gusta hacer?

3. ¿Dónde estás?

4. ¿Cuándo te despiertas? (you wake up)

5. ¿Cuándo te duermes? (you sleep)

6. ¿Cómo eres? (Remember that when this form of "*ser*" is used instead of "*estar*," it isn't asking how you are but rather for you to describe your characteristics).

Suggested Answers:

1. Yo soy Madelyn.

2. Me gusta ir al parque y me gusta visitar a mis amigos.

3. Estoy en mi casa.

4. Me despierto a las cuatro y media de la mañana.

5. Me duermo a las nueve de la noche.

6. Yo soy baja y rubia.

What You Do- Talking About Your Vocation
Career Vocabulary

Do you use *"ser"* or *"estar"* to talk about profession? Ser. Even though your profession can change, it is closer to "permanent" than "temporary" which is why we use the verb that is usually used for more permanent things. Below are some common professions and pronunciations.

Trabajo /trah-bah-ho/- work or job

Abogado /ah-bo-gah-do/- lawyer

Constructor /cun-strook-tor/- construction worker

Bombero /bohm-bear-oh/- fireman

Camarero /cahm-ah-rare-oh/- waiter

Dentista /den-tees-tuh/- dentist

Maestro /mah-ase-tro/- teacher

Piloto /pee-lo-to/- pilot

Peluquero /peh-loo-care-oh/- hairdresser

Médico /med-ee-co/- doctor

Secretario /seh-creh-tar-ee-oh/- secretary

Mecánico /meh-cahn-ee-co/- mechanic

Ingeniero /in-hen-ee-air-oh/- engineer

Jardinero /har-dee-nare-oh/- gardener

Cocinero /coh-see-nare-oh/- cook

Enfermero /en-fare-mare-oh/- nurse

Traductor /trah-dook-tor/- translator

Policía /po-lee-see-uh/- policeman/woman

Of the above professions, most of them can be changed to the femenine form by substituting the "*o*" on the end of "*a*." Of course, if it is fememine, you would use "*la*" instead of "*el*" at the beginning. "*Dentista*" and "*policia*" always have an "*a*" on the end whether it is a male or female. Look at the two sentences below.

La policía camina al parque.

El dentista trabaja diez horas.

You can see that the first sentence is talking about a policewoman and the second sentence is talking about a male dentist. The "*la*" or "*el*" is what shows the gender with those that don't change the ending.

With "*traductor*" and "*constructor*" that end in a consonant, you can make them femenine by adding an "*a*" onto the end. See the following two sentences.

El traductor no viene hoy.

La traductora viene a las dos y media.

The first sentence is about a male translator while the second sentence is about a female translator.

Asking and Answering about Jobs

There are several ways people might ask you about your job. Here are a few of the questions they might ask.

¿En qué trabajas?

¿Cuál es tu trabajo?

¿Qué haces?

The last question is more general and could be used in other circumstances as well. It can be asked when someone wants to know what you are currently doing or what you are doing in the future. *¿Qué haces mañana?*

Another question little kids might answer is.

¿Qué quieres ser cuando seas grande?

Here are some sample answers.

Quiero ser un bombero.

Quiero ser una dentista.

If someone were to ask you what you do, what would you answer?

Soy una maestra. Soy un policía.

Conversation Practice

Let's practice answering a few questions about both your profession and a friend's profession. Use full sentences to answer each question. Below the questions are sample conversations with sample answers that may or may not be similar to the ones you give.

¿En qué trabaja usted?

¿A usted le gusta su trabajo?

¿Qué le gusta sobre su trabajo?

¿Cuál es la profesión de su amigo?

¿A él le gusta su trabajo?

Sample conversations:

¿En qué trabaja usted?

Yo soy peluquero.

¿A usted le gusta su trabajo?

Si, me gusta mucho.

¿Qué le gusta sobre su trabajo?

Me gusta hablar con mis clientes.

¿Cuál es la profesión de su amigo?

Mi amigo es un doctor.

¿A él le gusta su trabajo?

Si, le gusta ser un doctor.

However, for now, another common question when talking about professions include the past perfect tense. You should memorize how to answer this type of question even though you haven't worked through this whole tense yet. That way, you will be prepared to answer it before having completed that verb study.

¿Cuánto tiempo has trabajado en la escuela? If you are a teacher, you might be asked this question.

¿Cuánto tiempo has trabajado en esta profesión? This question is more general and could be directed to anyone.

¿Cuánto tiempo has sido un _____*?* You would fill in the blank with your profession- médico, enfermero, ingeniero.

Your answer will use the same format. You will substitute "he" for "has" to change the question from asking about you to answering about I.

Yo he trabajado en la escuela por tres años.

Yo he trabajado en esta profesión por ocho meses.

Yo he sido un doctor por cuatro años.

You can see how the answers reflect the questions. You can pick one of these ways to answer and memorize the word order and format. That way, even if you aren't quite sure which format you are being asked, you can still answer the question correctly.

Where Are You Going?
The Verb "Ir"

The verb "*ir*" means to go, and it can be used to tell a place you are currently going. "Ir" being such a short verb has to be irregular. If you just took off the ending, you would be left with nothing. Below is a chart with the conjugation of "*ir*."

Yo voy	*Nosotros vamos*
Tú vas	*Vosotros vais*
Él/ ella/ usted va	*Ellos/ ustedes van*

While the verb is irregular, it still follows the ending pattern used with other verbs. You can see the "-*as*" ending with "*tú*" and so forth. When talking about a place you are going, you can make a sentence simply by picking the appropriate verb above and using "a" as well as the place.

For example,

Voy a mi casa.

Ella va a su casa.

Ellos van a su casa.

If you ever have a sentence like the following- *Yo voy a el parque*- you can combine "*a*" and "*el*." This combination is similar to the way we use conjugations. A + el = al

The correct way to say the above sentence is "*Yo voy **al** parque*." You wouldn't leave out "*el*" altogether and say "I go to park." That sounds stilted and awkward just as it does in

English. Note that if you are going to a femenine place, you will not combine "a" and "la." This combination only happens with "a" and "el."

Places Vocabulary

You have come across a few places so far in this book such as *"casa"* and *"parque,"* but you go many more places than that. Study the vocabulary list below and read the words aloud following the pronunciation list.

Iglesia /ee-gles-ee-uh/- church

Biblioteca /bee-blee-oh-tek-uh/- library

Dentista /den-tees-tuh/- dentist

Tienda /tee-en-duh/- store

Restaurante /res-tow-rahn-tay/- restaurant.

Cine /seen-ay/- movie theater

Playa /plai-yuh/- beach

Estación de bus /es-tah-see-on deh boos/- bus station

Mercado /mare-cah-do/- market

Farmacia /far-mah-see-uh/- pharmacy

Banco /bahn-co/- bank

Hospital /os-pee-tahl/- hospital

Panadería /pahn-ah-dare-ee-uh/- bakery

Librería /lee-brare-ree-uh/- bookstore

However, right now, you will simply be using the vocabulary to tell where you are going. Most of the above words are clearly either "el" or "la." However, a couple are a bit harder to guess.

Activity 1. Fill in the blanks below with either *el, la, los* or *las.*

_____ *playa*

_____ *mercado*

_____ *cine*

_____ *bancos*

_____ *farmacia*

_____ *hospitales*

_____ *librerias*

_____ *tienda*

_____ *estación de bus*

Answers-

La, el, el, los, la, los, las, la, la

Activity 2. Read the following statements and draw a picture that illustrates what is happening. The answers are below.

1. *Las niñas van a la playa.*

2. *Ellos van a la iglesia el domingo.*

3. *Yo voy a la estación de bus cada dia.*

55

    4. Mi padre va a la tienda.

Answers:

    1. The girls go to the beach.

    2. They go to the church on Sunday.

    3. I go to the bus station every day.

    4. My dad goes to the store.

Using "Ir" for the Future

Another way to use "*ir*" is to talk about something you are "going" to do. In English, we might say, "I am going to study." You can use the same format in Spanish. Read the following example sentences and figure out what each person is going to do.

Maria: Voy a visitar a mi abuela.

Jorge: Voy a comer carne y queso.

Pedro: Voy a nadar mañana.

This is the formula we use when using "ir" to talk about the future. "Conjugated Ir + a +unconjugated action."

Notice the second verbs in the above sentences. They are not conjugated. We do not say "*Voy a visito.*" That would be equivalent to saying "I am going I visit."

In fact, in other cases as well, if there are two verbs one after the other, the second verb is not conjugated. For example,

Necesito hablar. I need to speak. Once again, we would not say "I need I speak."

Quiero comer.

Ella quiere venir.

Activity 1. Read about their plans then answer the questions in full sentences. The answers can be found below.

Gregorio: El lunes, miércoles, y viernes, voy a trabajar. El martes, voy a jugar al tenis. Me gusta mucho jugar al béisbol, pero mi amigo no le gusta. El jueves, voy a limpiar mi casa. Y el sábado y domingo, voy a ir a la playa con mi familia.

Violeta: Necesito trabajar mucho esta semana. Trabajo cinco días a la semana- del martes al sábado. El domingo, voy a ir a la iglesia. El lunes, voy a la tienda y voy a comprar mucha comida, como arroz, frijoles, queso, y fruta. También, voy a llamar a mi amiga y hablar con ella. Y voy a caminar en el parque.

¿Qué va a hacer Gregorio el jueves?

¿Qué va a hacer Violeta el jueves?

¿Qué va a hacer Violeta el domingo?

¿Qué va a hacer Gregorio el viernes?

Respuestas (Answers):

Gregorio va a limpiar su casa.

Violeta va a trabajar el jueves.

Violeta va a ir a la iglesia el domingo.

Gregorio va trabajar el viernes.

Activity 2. Write about one thing you are going to do each day of the upcoming week. Here is an example schedule.

El lunes, voy a visitar a mi amiga.

El martes, voy a trabajar.

El miércoles, voy a ayudar a mi abuela.

El jueves, voy a comer una pizza grande.

El viernes, voy a mirar una película en el cine.

El sabado, voy a cocinar mucha comida.

El domingo, voy a ir a la iglesia.

Basic Conversations

Read the conversation aloud. Then, complete the second conversation with your own answers.

Elena: Hola, Marcos. ¿Cómo estás?

Marcos: Estoy bien, gracias. ¿Adonde vas?

Elena: Voy a la tienda para comprar comida para cenar. Necesito comprar huevos, fruta, carne, y repollo.

Marcos: Ah, ¿vas a hacer una ensalada?

Elena: Sí, voy a hacer una ensalada. ¿Quieres venir y comer la cena conmigo?

Marcos: No, no puedo. Voy a trabajar.

Elena: ¡Qué mal! Bueno, tal vez puedes venir a mi casa otro día.

Marcos: Okay, hasta luego.

Elena: Hasta luego.

Marcos: ¿Que vas a hacer hoy?

Tú:

Marcos: Yo voy a ir a la casa de mi amiga.

Tú:

Marcos: Sí, me gusta trabajar.

Tú:

Lightning Source UK Ltd.
Milton Keynes UK
UKHW020655210521
384116UK00005B/141

9 781802 148